S0-APN-261

SALT AND LIGHT
POCKET GUIDES

COMING TO GRIPS WITH MARITAL CONFLICT

COMING TO GRIPS WITH MARITAL CONFLICT

ERWIN W. LUTZER

MOODY PRESS

CHICAGO

© 1991 by
THE MOODY BIBLE INSTITUTE
OF CHICAGO

All rights reserved. No part of this book may
be reproduced in any form without permission in writing from the publisher, except in
the case of brief quotations embodied in critical articles or reviews.

All Scripture quotations, unless noted other-
wise, are from the *New American Standard Bible,* © 1960, 1962, 1963, 1968, 1971, 1972,
1973, 1975, and 1977 by The Lockman Foun-
dation, and are used by permission.

ISBN: 0-8024-3503-3

1 2 3 4 5 6 7 Printing/VP/Year 95 94 93 92 91

Printed in the United States of America

Coming to Grips with
MARITAL CONFLICT

He's so oppressive sometimes I think I'm in a concentration camp, and yet he expects to have sex with me! It's like a guard at Auschwitz wanting to have sex with a woman prisoner and expecting her to enjoy it!"

With all of her might this woman tried to be the good Christian wife she was taught to be. For years she lived with a demanding, hot-tempered husband, trusting God to change him. But her submission seemed to have little effect on his attitude and actions. Her question was one that many married partners ask: When is enough, enough?

Although the male species at times may seem to be the most difficult to live with, many women make impossible demands on their husbands, thereby blocking all possible avenues to harmony and mutual respect. "Everything I do is wrong," a man told me. "I receive no affirmation, she is constantly undermining my authority, and hates sex. Some day I would like to catch her in a good mood!"

No one plans to have an unhappy marriage. Yet marital conflict exists everywhere. Even those who appear to have a fulfilling marriage often live with anger, mistrust, and disharmony. Many wives say they have no one to talk to, they are neglected, and despair of finding help even after years of struggle. Husbands in turn complain that they are weary of being nagged, weary of being compared to Robert Redford, and exasperated when their wives accuse them of being sexual animals.

We would be startled if we knew the amount of verbal and even physical abuse that goes on in homes. Yes, even Christian homes. When the curtains are drawn, only God knows what happens behind the closed doors. And for the most part, it's not a pretty picture. If marriage is to mirror the relationship between Christ and the Church then many (most?) marriages are a tragic failure. Surely God intended something better.

Marital conflict is as old as the human race. But our "fallenness" is having a greater impact on this generation. Look no farther than your daily newspaper and you will see the symptoms of marital discord.

CAUSES OF CONFLICT

Why all this conflict? Five factors contribute to discord in marriage: the fractured family, unrealistic expectations, sexual immorality, an inadequate understanding of conflict, and the belief that change is impossible.

THE FRACTURED FAMILY

Ever since Cain killed Abel, broken homes have existed, with abuse and hatred spilling into the lives of the children. But thirty years ago here in the United States, this breakdown began to permeate all areas of society—rich and poor, black and white, educated and uneducated. Divorce, which always carried the stigma of failure, now is a popular and sophisticated escape from an unhappy marriage. The social restraints that encouraged people to work out their problems have disappeared.

Children caught in the midst of rejection and power plays have grown up without the warm and secure relationships they crave. They have lacked role models and have been unable to cope with the hostility they have felt toward a father, a mother, or both.

With the proliferation of pornography, sexual molestation and abuse have escalated. We are told that one in four girls will be sexually abused by a father, a relative, or a trusted neighbor.[1] Sexual aberrations of various kinds are common.

Unless these emotional wounds are resolved, rejected children enter marriage with a huge bundle of emotional deficiencies and oppressive feelings—feelings bound to spill over into the most intimate of all relationships. Those who have their roots in a dysfunctional family often are unable to give or receive love. Far from curing such deficiencies, marriage actually brings such problems to light.

I'm not suggesting that those who have had a deprived childhood have no chance for marital harmony, but they may have to work harder to achieve fulfillment in their marriage relationship. Thankfully, God helps people minimize, if not totally negate, the power of a destructive past.

UNREALISTIC EXPECTATIONS

Incredibly, some people actually expect marriage to make them happy! Of course, marriage does bring happiness, but only to those who have already found meaning in their personal relationship with God. In other words, those who are unhappy single will likely be unhappy married.

Some women think that God created their husbands for the sole purpose of making them (the wives) happy. When this doesn't happen, they chip away at their husbands, trying to shape the kind of person who makes them happy. Unfortunately, their best efforts often backfire, and the door to progress slams shut.

I've known engaged couples who were clearly mismatched, but thought that after marriage their problems would vanish. Too late they discovered that their differences were increased tenfold. Like a magnifying glass, marriage took manageable irritations and enlarged them.

As a path to happiness marriage is overrated. Two imperfect people cannot come together without mutual disappointments and struggles. If this is so for those who are emotionally well-adjusted, think of the implications for the young man or woman who marries simply to get away from home, or for a couple with only marginal emotional and spiritual stability. "If love is blind," someone observed, "marriage is an eye opener!" Those who think marriage is a shortcut to happiness will wish they had taken the main road.

Marriage cannot do what only God can; that is, bring inner contentment. Marriage is at best two imperfect people, united in body, soul, and spirit in a growing relationship that is to reflect the unity of the Godhead. Every marriage has its stresses, which can be used either to unite the couple or to divide them.

SEXUAL IMMORALITY

Moral impurity sows seeds that eventually can bear bitter fruit. Many couples who do not know how to neutralize the detrimental effects of premarital sex significantly reduce their chances for a happy marriage. Some couples say that they enjoyed sex before marriage, but their relationship went sour immediately after saying "I do." Before marriage they could enjoy sex without resolving deeper issues in their relationship. Real matters of communication and honest differences were buried under artificial intimacy. Marriage forced them to deal with these pressure points. Add to this the mistrust that developed because of their past relationship, and all the ingredients for conflict are present.

Of course there is cleansing and forgiveness for past sexual relationships. But unless the past has been fully faced in the presence of God, a couple that has had premarital relationships will be living with unfinished business.

In a companion booklet, *Coming to Grips with Your Sexual Past,* I discuss further the effects of promiscuity and abuse. One must honestly confront his or her sexual past for trust and mutual respect to thrive in marriage. Thankfully, Christ can "break the power of canceled sin," to quote the words of Charles Wesley.

AN INADEQUATE
UNDERSTANDING OF CONFLICT

Many of us were taught to believe that if we "married the right one" we would be free of all marital conflict and would live out our days in uninterrupted harmony and fulfillment.

This is a myth, of course, since God often uses conflict as a means of spiritual growth. How best can God teach us to love except to put us into a relationship where that love is severely tested? How can He teach us patience and the inner resources of joy, except in a marriage where there will be disappointment and misunderstanding? How can He teach us forgiveness except to put us in a relationship where we will have to extend forgiveness as well as receive it?

A Britisher, when told that there were many divorces in America based on incompatibility, replied, "I thought that incompatibility is the purpose of marriage!" After all, when two self-willed people live together in the most intimate of all relationships, what else can we expect except incompatibility?

Obviously I'm not suggesting that an unmarried person should seek an incompatible partner. But once the marriage has taken place, couples should see their conflicts as part of God's training program, teaching them the deeper lessons of God's power even in the midst of their difficulties and failures.

Those who avoid conflict often live with a superficial harmony that never confronts the real issues in the relationship.

THE BELIEF THAT CHANGE IS IMPOSSIBLE

Our disappointments with ourselves and others often leave us with the depressing conclusion that difficulties within a marriage cannot be resolved. Apart from a few cosmetic adjustments, we don't believe that God is able to make a radical change in a mate's attitude and disposition.

But if both the husband and the wife are Christians, they have powerful resources to bring about the love and respect needed for a satisfying relationship. If we say that God cannot bring about such changes, we call His integrity into question. Did He not promise that the Holy Spirit would re-produce the love and power of Christ within us? If the Son shall make us free, are we not "free indeed" (John 8:36)?

God is able to transform those who come from a dysfunctional family, those who have committed immorality, or who are filled with anger —He is able to bring about a transformation that is both deep and lasting. There is a price, of course, and that is the willingness to be honest enough to face oneself in the presence of God. More of that later.

As a pastor, I have seen couples struggle through years of conflict; yet they gradually deepened their relationship and love. Against incredible odds, some have persevered to see harmony, respect, and fulfillment.

Unfortunately, I've seen many of the other kind as well. I have watched relationships disintegrate, partners persist in adultery or abuse, and children scarred by divorce, resentment, and rejection. I've seen marriages, believed to be made in heaven, unravel here on earth.

The difference between success or failure doesn't depend on the depth of the problems, for some of the most hopeless marriages have been turned around for the better. The difference is that one couple opened their lives to the power of Christ and another did not. Some couples faced the pain of their personal failures whereas others would not pay the price that honesty required.

Logic alone does not help us achieve harmony in marriage. A man who believes he can manage his marriage with reason and hard-headed negotiations will probably be judged as a failure by his wife and children. Most issues in marriage are primarily matters of feeling, and not of rational considerations. That's why genuine change always involves pain. Happily married couples have learned to respect one another's feelings, even though they cannot understand the whys and the wherefores.

There is hope for unhappy marriages, but it does take the cooperation of both partners. Even those who live with a difficult mate or a mate who feels that he/she has cooperated and the other partner is at fault can find hope through scriptural principles. And yes, even when the fight to save the marriage appears hopeless, the Bible gives hope and help.

PRINCIPLES FOR RESOLVING CONFLICT

Here are seven principles that will help resolve the roots of many conflicts that, from time to time, are found in most marriages. Any desper-

ate couple can apply them for themselves.

Although it takes two to generate
strife, blame for marital friction is
usually not an equal fifty-fifty. One
partner usually bears greater responsibility for the failure of the marriage.
But seldom is one partner wholly responsible.

Our tendency to see other peo-
ples' faults more clearly than our own
is so deeply rooted in our nature that
Jesus used this humorous illustration
to get his point across. He said, "And
why do you look at the speck that is
in your brother's eye, but do not no-
tice the log that is in your own eye?
Or how can you say to your brother,
'Let me take the speck out of your
eye' and behold, the log is in your own
eye?" (Matthew 7:3-4). The irony is
obvious: Visualize a person trying to
take out a splinter from his brother's
eye when he has a block of wood in
his own!

Put a pencil in a glass of water
and it will appear crooked. In the
same way, our perception of others,
and especially our perception of ourselves are always skewed. To see ourselves for what we are is so painful
that many of us build elaborate de-

15

fenses for our own insecurities and shortcomings. Anger, pride, and selfishness cause us to see everyone else (particularity our marriage partner) as "bent."

Recall when King David committed adultery, Nathan the prophet came to him with a story about a rich man who stole a lamb from his poor neighbor. Incredibly, David said that the rich man should be put to death. Not once did he realize that this was a picture of himself taking Bathsheba from another man when he (David) already had many wives. David showed more compassion for a lamb than he did for Uriah, one of his most trusted and mighty soldiers! He could see someone else's faults with 20/20 vision but was blind toward his own.

Ask each partner in a marriage to list the faults of the other and they will do so quickly (often requesting more paper). Ask them to list the strengths of the other and there will be long pauses, as they grudgingly list one or two items.

Denial is the most common barrier to facing ourselves in the presence of God. There are those who simply will not admit that they are abusive, unreasonable, controlling, or angry. Often through years of rationalization, some partners have insulated themselves from seeing themselves as they truly are.

Some men hate women and use the marriage relationship to vent their anger. Such a man may be wholly unconscious of this rage and in counseling will appeal to the biblical command "Wives, submit yourselves to your husbands" to justify his actions. His hostility is proved by the constant need to control his wife. One day she can spend money and he congratulates her; the next day he flies into a rage, throwing her purchases on the floor. This unpredictability is his way of exerting control; he makes sure his wife is always off balance. In his need for control, he will hold his wife to an impossible standard to ensure that she will fail. This then gives him the right to be critical, angry, and even abusive.

Such a man lives in a cocoon called denial. Years of rationalization have clouded his perception. Nothing can change his perspective, for it is necessary for him to always be right. His wife may also have taken flight from reality. She may be deceived by his occasional "nice" behavior. She will think, "After all, he does love me," and so she convinces herself that next time it will be different. Often she will play the role of the martyr, overnurturing, overcaring, believing that she is called to be the one to rescue her wayward husband. Usually, such a woman will take full blame for her husband's ill treatment and think that he will improve if only she does better next time. All the while she does not face up to the deep unresolved needs that prevent him from giving and receiving love.

Of course, many variations exist to the above scenario. The wife may seek to control her husband through manipulation, bad moods, and threats. She may deliberately set up barriers in their relationship so that when her husband becomes angry she can blame all their disputes on him. Because she cannot receive his love she unconsciously makes it impossible for her husband to love her. If she fears intimacy, she will make sure that her marriage is in a constant state of conflict so that she can deny sex to her husband.

In these kinds of marriages, there is a fundamental unwillingness to confront the deep roots of anger, rejection, and insecurity. Let's admit that at some time all of us have been self-deceived. We actually think we are being reasonable when we are not, we believe we are thoughtful when we are manipulative, and we believe we are loving when all that we care about is our own needs.

Some partners have lived with denial for so long that they cannot benefit from any spiritual counsel. All correction is dismissed with hostile rationalizations. Sometimes only a traumatic event will awaken them so that they can see themselves with a degree of objectivity.

A second defense mechanism is *projection*, the tendency to attribute to others the faults that we ourselves have. For example, a person who is angry may accuse his mate of anger; the controlling person may accuse his mate of wanting to exercise control. The very traits we attribute to others may be the ones that dominate our lives.

This is why two people who are alike often have so much friction in marriage. They cannot tolerate what they see in their mates simply because they cannot bear to see themselves. One husband reluctantly came to me after his wife complained that he had verbally and physically abused her. He in turn accused her of being angry and controlling simply because she complained about his abuse! Any kind of resistance was seen as a threat to his authority.

Because we are sinful creatures who love darkness rather than light, we seek to escape the light of the truth. We come to a confrontation armed with our rationalizations, our perceptions, and our most believable lies. Only honesty before God can penetrate the walls that insulate us from needed change.

True marital harmony requires us to evaluate honestly who we really are and how we react to those around us. Often this requires the presence of a counselor, who can help each mate see himself/herself as the other perceives him.

But counselors can only go so far. God must break into our souls so that we are able to see ourselves as God sees us apart from Christ. Marital harmony can only begin when we pray with David, "Search me, O God, and know my heart; try me and know my anxious thoughts; and see if there be any hurtful way in me, and lead me in the everlasting way" (Psalm 139:23-24).

One warning, though: Some people who are open and honest about themselves still will exhibit little positive change. They persuade themselves that honesty itself is their ticket to acceptance and the forgiveness of their mate. Honesty becomes a substitute for true repentance and change. "I'm having an affair, but at least I'm honest about it," is an extreme example of the kind of subtle justification that honesty sometimes produces.

Honesty, then, can become a permanent excuse for obstinate behavior. One woman who experienced some childhood abuse used this as an excuse for not having intercourse with her husband. She felt justified in refusing him because of the trauma of her youth. Rather than using her past as an opportunity for growth, it became a convenient peg that held all the excuses she used to not respond in sexual intimacy.

Of course, an honest self-examination is only the first step in resolving marital conflict. Honesty should become a doorway to healing. The open sores of the past should become fading scars, proving that healing has taken place. The purpose of such an examination is not to find a reason why we are in conflict but to discover how we can leave the past behind and become emotionally whole.

What if one partner refuses to allow God to do a thorough spiritual examination? Let that not be an excuse for the other to hold back in such openness toward God. Sometimes when one partner changes the other does also, though there are no guarantees.

One partner can grow spiritually in a marriage even if the other does not. Indeed, some of the most measured growth in our lives happens when we are enclosed with God, unable to depend on any human being for our spiritual nourishment. Our disappointment in our mate often "crowds us to Christ," to borrow a phrase from L. E. Maxwell. To those who think that changes on their part will not bring about changes in their mate, I respond, "Give God a chance ... and even if there are no observable results, think of how we honor God when we show love to those who do not return it."

Resolving marital conflict begins with honest self-examination so that forgiveness can take place. Through such honesty God wounds us that He might heal us. He breaks us that He might put us back together.

Growth Assignment:
1. In the presence of God confess your shortcomings and failures: anger, selfishness, moral impurity, a critical spirit.
2. Ask God to give you the appropriate time to confess these failures to your mate.
3. Give your partner to God without any thought of changing him/her through your own efforts.

THE CLARIFICATION OF ROLES

Contemporary society insists that the roles of men and women are interchangeable. Such a move toward equality, it is argued, will minimize the abuse that women have had to endure because of male domination. Some Christians, unduly caught up by the spirit of the age, have actually attempted to interpret the Bible to make it agree with these secular attitudes.

But there are important reasons that God gave men and women different roles in the marriage relationship. To quote Paul, "But as the church is subject to Christ, so also the wives ought to be to their husbands in everything" (Ephesians 5:24). This text, and others like it, are balanced by the responsibilities given to husbands: "Husbands, love your wives, just as Christ also loved the church and gave Himself up for her" (v. 25).

The responsibility of the husband is headship; that is, giving leadership to his wife and children. He should not do this, however, without consulting his wife and serving her and his children. He is responsible for all decisions affecting the direction and care of the home. To exercise leadership does not imply that he must always get his own way. It does mean that he should take the good of the family into account in the decisions that are made.

The role of the wife is submission to her husband's leadership. The Greek word is *hupotasso*, which literally means "to get under the burden of" someone. A wife should get under the burden of her husband, to make choices that affirm her husband as the leader. She understands his goals and aspirations and commits herself to seeing them fulfilled. In a word, *hupotasso* means submission.

Interestingly, nowhere in the New Testament is a man instructed to force his wife to submit to him. The implication seems to be that if the husband treats his wife with love and respect, her submission will grow out of their relationship. Many decisions should be made together, without an appeal to the lines of authority. Just as elders should not "lord it over" those who are to submit to their authority, so the husband should not "lord it over" his wife.

To dilute these biblical roles is to invite more conflict, not less. Recently I heard of one woman who has divorced twice and is now dating another man, looking for "equality in the relationship." Equality, however, will be more likely to destroy a relationship that to build it.

Unless a couple has talked through their understanding of roles in the relationship, disagreements will escalate until the relationship will break under its own weight. Without clarifying expectations, there is little hope of harmony.

What constitutes unwarranted control by a husband in a marriage relationship? Some women do not mind living with a man who has high expectations and gives detailed instructions about virtually everything.

Other women resent such intrusion, feeling they are being treated like a child. They insist that they want space and enjoy measured independence. They understand that the husband has the final say in all important decisions in the marriage, but they expect to make the decisions about clothing, food, and the myriad details that pertain to the children. Where that invisible line should be drawn must be decided by every couple.

Is the wife ever justified in choosing to "not submit"? Does there come a point when the demands of her husband are so unreasonable that she should stand her ground? The question of how a wife should respond in such situations will be discussed at the end of this booklet.

What is God's prescription for marital harmony? *The wife must submit to the husband's authority, and the husband should love her with the gentleness of Christ.* Though he bears the ultimate responsibility in the home, he should also submit to her by putting his emotional and spiritual shoulder under her burden and helping her in every way he can.

Think of the harmony that would exist if each partner sincerely tried to lighten the load of his/her spouse. The fight for control would dissipate if each sought the good of the other. Many couples go into marriage without having defined what their expectations are. The man may think that his wife will accept the role that his mother had; the wife may have a perspective based on what she observed in her home, or possibly an ideal drawn from her own imagination.

How often I have seen the wife take the role of the husband because of his own negligence. This appears to work, but in the long run it destroys the marriage by rewarding his weakness.

Blessed is the couple that can discuss openly their expectations of what each is obligated to do within the marriage relationship. Unless these roles are clarified, conflict is bound to exist.

Growth Assignment:
1. With the help of a commentary, study Ephesians 5:22-33. Honestly discuss the expectations you have of one another.
2. Talk through the different perspectives you have regarding the roles each should play. Talk about your family backgrounds, trying to understand who shaped your views of the marriage relationship.

MEANINGFUL COMMUNICATION

Every couple that lives with marital discord has a problem with communication. That word *communication* refers to the ability to share both verbally and nonverbally so that the message is accepted and understood. Many couples hear only words that trigger various emotional reactions, but they do not understand what is really being said. Wives often complain, "He simply does not listen to what I am saying . . . he doesn't understand the depth of my feelings and hurt." The husband may be shocked when he comes home to discover that she has run away; he didn't realize that she was near the breaking point.

A strong love relationship is not possible without communication. When couples lock one another out of their hearts they communicate only superficially, failing to understand or appreciate what the other is trying to say. They are miles apart in the same house. Soon each wears a "Keep Out" sign over the heart.

Hear the heart cry of one woman: "I feel like a thing. Is my conversation so unintelligible that I am not worth talking to? I could be a post in the ground for all he bothers to communicate with me. All of a sudden I feel like I don't even know my husband. It's as if he has been hiding from me for years."

What makes a person (usually the man) unwilling to reveal who he really is? What makes it nigh impossible to share his innermost struggles and thoughts with his wife?

The first reason is shame, the sense of humiliation that comes when the truth is exposed. After all, none of us would like to have our inmost thoughts revealed. And if some private acts have accompanied those private thoughts, exposure becomes even more dreadful.

Along with shame is fear of rejection. "If my wife really knew me, she could never love me," one man put it simply. But most women would prefer to know the truth from their husbands than to wonder what really goes on beneath that cold, impersonal exterior. It is difficult to love someone whose life is partially hidden, someone who resembles "The Great Stone Face."

A third reason is the realization that changes must take place once the truth is out. A man has a secret romance, or a woman spends more money than her husband knows about —these and a dozen other similar issues must be confronted when communication begins once again.

Some people put all their communication on "auto pilot," bypassing their emotions. Talking in depth about their feelings and fears simply is too painful. This is particularly true of those who have suffered abuse years earlier.

Communication, meaningful communication, requires *trust*. Imagine the surprise one wife received when she came home unexpectedly to find her husband dressed in women's clothes, including undergarments! As the truth began to unfold, she discovered that he had been a transvestite for many years without her knowing it. Understandably, it will take a long time before this woman trusts her husband again. No matter how deep their communication, there will be the suspicion that another surprise may be around the corner.

Immorality, a secret life of pornography, and involvement in shady business practices—these and other such revelations damage the trust that is necessary for spiritual unity. Trust can return, but it must be earned through honesty and accountability.

The second requirement for meaningful communication is *respect*. Every time a partner loses his/her temper and uses words to hurt, something in the relationship is lost that will have to be regained. Most marriages have pressure points that are scrupulously avoided because they become the focal point of so much anger that eventually the issues are bypassed and left unresolved. Sex, money, the relatives, children—these matters are simply ignored until they rupture in an outburst of anger and deep hostility.

Unfortunately, many couples attempt to communicate at the wrong time and in the wrong way. Most arguments take place because important issues are discussed under pressure rather than at a time that is calm, free from the immediate context of the disagreement. Couples who do not take time to talk about their differences before they erupt will soon tolerate destructive communication as a part of the daily routine.

Communication can only take place when each mate attempts to honestly look at the issues from the other's point of view. We cannot understand what the other person is feeling unless we are willing to "walk a mile in our mate's sandals."

Growth Assignment:
1. Prove the power of words by choosing to speak only positive words to your mate for one week.
2. Choose to talk about one of the "untouchables," those issues usually avoided because they spark heated disagreement.
3. Ask your partner to define his/her need. Then seek to meet it.

Many partners enter marriage totally unaware of the basic differences that exist between a man and a woman. Peter admonished husbands, "You husbands live with your wives in an understanding way, as with a weaker vessel, since she is a woman; and grant her honor as a fellow heir of the grace of life, so that your prayers may not be hindered" (1 Peter 3:7).

What should husbands know about women? They must understand that most women look to their husbands for affirmation, both for their accomplishments and their physical beauty. They desire to know that they are number one in their husband's priorities. Wives want physical affection, not just as a prelude to sex but as a constant affirmation of mutual love and attraction. They want their husbands to understand the burdens they bear and for them to spend time in communication. Usually sensitive, wives often are deeply hurt by half truths, irresponsibility, and passive leadership.

Similarly, women must try to understand the burdens and aspirations of their husbands. They must also understand the powerful sexual temptations their husbands face. One woman lashed out in judgmental anger when she found a pornographic magazine in her husband's desk. This only drove her husband deeper into the world of pornography, determined to hide his magazines more carefully!

If she had approached him with love, trying to understand the power of this temptation, he might have been willing to express his inner struggles. Such communication might have been an important first step to victory over his secret vice. And if the habit continued, he would have been more open to seeking professional help. Unfortunately, a judgmental, self-righteous rebuke broke the communication.

One day a man called me on the phone, revealing that he had been involved in immorality but could not possibly ask his wife for forgiveness because she had always warned him, "If you ever commit adultery, I will never have you back!" Apparently she thought that her warning would be a deterrent, but actually it only drove the man away from his wife at the very moment he needed her the most.

Peter has some important words for Christian wives who are married to unsaved husbands. After he describes Christ's obedience to the cross, he continues, "In the same way, you wives, be submissive to your own husbands so that even if any of them are disobedient to the word, they may be won without a word by the behavior of their wives, as they observe your chaste and respectful behavior" (1 Peter 3:1-2).

When a woman's husband does not obey the Word, the wife is to exhibit a meek spirit of submission. This may lead him to Christ. (Peter probably is thinking about an unsaved man, though the principle would apply to a carnal Christian husband too.)

Peter understands a basic trait of the male human nature, namely, that men are usually not influenced spiritually by the verbal witness of their wives. Call it male macho, or pride, the fact is men are seldom converted when their wives assume the role of evangelist.

One woman said that when Billy Graham was on television she pushed the portable TV in front of her husband "to give him a good dose of Billy Graham." Another woman's attempt to convert her husband backfired when she painted "REPENT" on the bottom of his beer can. His friends were over to watch a football game and her husband was hardly impressed when they saw the not so subtle message! He is a believer today and can laugh about it now, but at the time he was not amused.

Peter does not promise that the husband will be saved as a result of the submission of the wife. Certainly, her Christlike spirit will be more likely to bring a change of heart, but it is not guaranteed. Many stories can be told of how wives through their gracious submission have won their husbands to Christ.

Beyond the basic differences between a man and a woman, the two bring distinct personal differences to marriage. Tragically, some of the most minor differences of perspective can cloud a marriage if one or both partners is unwilling to give the other "space," the opportunity to be different even at the personal inconvenience of the other.

To live with mutual understanding is to live with the knowledge that marital conflicts are inevitable. Fortunately, these conflicts can be minimized as each partner seeks to understand the other, making allowance for differences of lifestyle and attitude. Partners who seek understanding do not feel the necessity of squeezing their partner into their own mold.

In his book *What Wives Wish Their Husbands Knew About Women* (Tyndale House, 1977), James Dobson describes many of the differences between males and females. Blessed are those who are continually growing in mutual understanding and acceptance of their mates.

Growth Assignment:
1. Make a covenant to read 1 Corinthians 13 each day until you can quote it from memory.
2. Trust the Holy Spirit to reproduce those qualities in your life.

FORGIVENESS

All happily married people have learned to forgive. In our fallen world, each of us has been disappointed in our mate. The person who cannot forgive is the person who will not be able to truly love. One measure of the strength of a relationship is the length of time that passes before a couple will reconcile to one another after an argument. I can only pity the married person who cannot utter those simple words, "I'm sorry, will you forgive me?"

When there has been a breach of trust, certain steps must be taken to effect reconciliation. Here are two basic principles to bring emotional unity to a ruptured relationship.

First, *reconciliation can only take place when the offending party asks for forgiveness.* While it is possible for a marriage to survive when one partner "forgives" without being asked, eventually the relationship will become strained. Christ said, "Be on your guard! If your brother sins, rebuke him; and if he repents, forgive him"

(Luke 17:3). If the offender is unwilling to humbly admit failure and express a desire to be forgiven, the other mate cannot pretend that life is to continue as if nothing happened. Barriers can only be broken by a spirit of reconciliation.

One woman told me that her husband did not ask her for forgiveness when his adulterous relationship was discovered. He acted as if this infraction was not as serious as his wife made it out to be. By minimizing the affair, he showed an unwillingness to come to terms with his destructive behavior. As a result, it was difficult for his wife to put the incident behind her, pretending that this was but a minor bump along the marital road.

What should a woman do whose husband is unwilling to face the reality of his disobedience? There is no one correct answer to this question. Obviously, a qualified pastor or counselor must become involved to bring the offender to accountability. To allow such behavior to continue will only perpetuate, not solve, the problems in the relationship.

Second, *once forgiveness has been granted, it cannot be revoked.* Paul wrote, "And be kind to one another, tender-hearted, forgiving each other, just as God in Christ also has forgiven you" (Ephesians 4:32). How does

God forgive us? He takes our sins and throws them into the depths of the sea and remembers them no more (Micah 7:19, Jeremiah 31:34).

One man told me how he humbly confessed his infidelity to his wife. Although she initially said that she would forgive him, she refused to forget. Years later whenever they had a disagreement she would remind him of the past. "For years she rubbed my nose in the dirt" he told me. Though this couple lived together sexually, in their spirits they were never reconciled. This is not forgiveness!

Counselors disagree about whether an adulterous partner should even confess infidelity to the other. Since in some cases the relationship seems irrevocably damaged, the argument is that the offender should simply deal with it on his or her own, or with the help of a counselor. However, I believe it is much better that a partner find out about the relationship directly rather than from a secondary source. Because news of infidelity eventually surfaces, it is generally best that the offender break the news to the other partner. One woman I know was exceedingly angry when she discovered that everyone knew about her husband's affair except she herself! Also, think of the damage done if in withholding this information, one's partner contracts a sexually transmitted disease as a result of the liaison.

"Is the repentance genuine?" Often those partners who are expected to forgive a flagrant moral infraction ask that question. We must remember that those who practice abuse, immorality, or other aberrations may be sincere in their repentance, but, remember, *a change in behavior takes much more than one act of renunciation.* These sins are like alcoholism; they can be sworn off, only to resurface. Many a sincere wife has erred in thinking that her husband will now be different because he tearfully begged for forgiveness. There is a bonding to abuse, immorality, and dishonesty. No matter how sincere the repentance, tomorrow is another day.

Repentance must therefore include several safeguards that are built into the relationship. First, there is accountability. Where there has been a flagrant violation, a third party (a pastor, a counselor, or group) must be brought into the situation to insure that the future will be different from the past. In many instances a couple simply cannot handle these matters on their own.

Second, steps must be taken to aid in spiritual and emotional growth. There must be evidence that this partner (or both) is willing to actively pursue those things that produce harmony rather than betrayal.

Third, because of the special bonding to sin, the partners must always be on guard lest the same cycle of behavior reappear.

Partners must ask God for wisdom in steering a course between resisting reconciliation and the opposite extreme of naively accepting an intention to do better as a valid reason to believe that the past behavior will never resurface.

Forgiveness and reconciliation must become a part of every marriage and particularly those where trust has been badly damaged. Only when barriers crumble can a marriage be restored.

Growth Assignment:
1. Ponder the parable of Christ in Matthew 18:21-35.
2. Apply this teaching on forgiveness to your own marriage. How can this teaching change your marriage?

SATANIC CONFLICT

Many marriages will never be harmonious until the couple understands the role of demonic spirits in building barriers to marriage fulfillment.

Of course, there would be conflict even if Satan did not exist, because our sinful nature has the seeds of all the sins that mitigate against harmony and love. But Satan takes those sins and strengthens their power so that the ruts become deeper, the barriers become higher, and the differences appear more hopeless.

One man lived with a woman who would often undergo a change in personality, often in a few moments of time. They would be out shopping in relative harmony, then on the way home she would be, in his words, "transformed into a different person." She would erupt suddenly in anger, false accusations, and threats. He quickly realized that she was oppressed by an evil spirit and so began fervent prayer to rebuke this influence. He quietly enlisted the prayer support of many Christian friends, and as a result she has started on the path to emotional stability.

Sometimes when sin enters into a marriage relationship, the effects can bring a whole new set of conflicts. One woman had an affair with a man whom she had known sexually before her marriage. Her husband was crushed when he discovered the relationship, and he began a long battle of spiritual warfare. He became so angry he eventually was oppressed by evil spirits, and he began to abuse his wife. Because she had repented of the relationship, she had authority to address the spirits directly to protect her own life. Without her husband's knowledge she enlisted other believers to pray and experienced significant results. After she had entered a room to pray and rebuke the spirits, she often returned to find her husband subdued, wondering why he had acted as he did.

In answer to prayer, God protected the children from knowing what was happening in the home. In her letter she said, "The battle appears to be over. My husband is one of the most Christlike men I know. We pray together and he is leading our children spiritually."

I do not tell these stories to imply that all women should live with an abusive husband. Nor do I think that with the proper amount and intensity of intercession all abusive husbands will inevitably be transformed into even-tempered men of God. And not all abuse derives from the presence of evil spirits. But when spirit-influence exists, *we must remember evil spirits do all that they can to drive wedges between a man and his wife.* A marriage with deep problems seldom finds resolution without overcoming direct satanic conflict.

Satan is persistent. He wants to wear us down, to bring us to the point of exhaustion so that we will simply give up and walk out of a situation. (For a good primer on spiritual warfare, read *The Adversary* [Moody Press, 1975], by Mark Bubeck.)

Growth Assignment:
1. Think of as many sins as you can that give Satan a foothold in your marriage.
2. With a commentary, study James 4:1-11 and respond to whatever God shows you through this passage.
3. Pray against Satan's attempt to destroy your marriage.

A TIME FOR SEPARATION

The Bible is silent about what should be done if a husband treats his wife cruelly, either with physical abuse or by asking her to compromise her convictions. Nor does it give specific instructions on how to handle adultery, alcoholism, or child abuse.

The Bible also says that children should obey their parents, and no exceptions are listed . But I must ask: Is a child violating the intention of this command if he tells his teacher that he and his siblings are being abused at home—has he violated Scripture if he was expressly told by his father to keep the abuse of the children a family secret? I think not.

I believe there are times when a person's loyalty to God supersedes one's loyalty to God-ordained social structures. It is unlikely that either Peter or Paul would have expected no exceptions to wives' submission to husbands. If there are times when we do not expect a child to obey his parents (as when asked to remain quite about abuse), there may be times when a wife is no longer expected to obey an oppressive husband. And even if a wife can endure the abuse, what should she do when children are involved? How vividly I recall a woman saying to me, "I could continue to live with him even if he kills me, but I must leave because of what he is doing to my children."

Should a woman who is commanded by her husband to commit adultery (say, for the sake of pleasing a superior) do it in the name of submission? Should she participate in occult rituals just because her husband demands it? Should she keep her husband's abuse of the children a secret just to protect him? Similarly, must a husband live with an adulterous or abusive wife? These are the forces that are tearing marriages apart, leaving little hope for lasting restoration.

In the Bible there are instances where God's people have disobeyed some human authority and have been approved by God for doing so. The midwives of Egypt, Daniel, and the apostles all chose to obey God rather than men. Grudem writes that these passages mean we should "obey except when it would be a sin to obey."[2]

Paul the apostle was realistic enough to know that there are times when couples may have to separate, even if this act does not involve the next step of divorce. "But to the married I give instructions, not I, but the Lord, that the wife should not leave her husband (but if she does leave, let her remain unmarried, or else be reconciled to her husband), and that the husband should not send the wife away" (1 Corinthians 7:10-11).

Each partner should evaluate his/her situation with the help of a godly counselor. There must be a balance, I believe, between the suffering that all of us should be willing to endure for the sake of our partner (and Christ) and the eventual line crossed when the marriage simply is beyond meaningful redemption.

A legal separation differs from a divorce in that the intent is to have legal protection without needing to finally end the marriage. This also allows the possibility of reconciliation (as Paul taught). If it is necessary to take the second step of divorce for the purposes of custody, or a similarly strong reason, the Christian partner should understand that this does not necessarily mean that the marriage bond is broken in the sight of God. Such a divorce may protect both partners' rights, but it does not necessarily give them the right to remarry.

Those of us who believe there are "grounds for divorce" admit that the Bible gives evidence for only two, namely, sexual infidelity and desertion. In such cases, remarriage would then be justified. But the Bible gives no other such grounds. Therefore, if a divorce takes place on the grounds of alcoholism or abuse, for example, the believer who has obtained that divorce has no right to remarry. Such a divorce has not broken the original marriage bond. The divorce is simply the means used to take advantage of civil laws.

I know a woman who obtained a divorce because her husband was abusing her children. She realized, however, that this divorce did not break the marriage covenant in the eyes of God. Thus she has chosen to live as a single woman, free only to remarry in the event of her husband's death or his own remarriage (in which case he would break the marriage bond through adultery).

Other pastors/scholars may have different ways to resolve these difficult problems. Each mate must struggle to his/her own conclusion believed to be consistent with the Bible and conscience.

Too many couples look to divorce as a convenient escape. In doing so, they circumvent the suffering that God would use in their lives as a means of spiritual refinement. If separation and divorce become necessary, they always are a *tragic* necessity.

Growth Assignment:

1. Give yourself and your marriage to God and trust Him to do a miracle so that you will be obedient to His will, and His will alone.
2. Be willing to suffer in your marriage for the sake of Christ to whatever extent God may desire. (Read 1 Peter once each day for one week.)

KEEPING THE PEACE

I conclude with this reminder: *It is possible for one partner to live a godly, dedicated life even if the other is contentious.* Consider the forbearance of the famous English evangelist John Wesley, the founder of the Methodist church. One day he met a young woman, Grace, who appeared to be everything he could ever want in a wife. She was spiritually minded and had a heart for ministry. She even enjoyed horseback riding, and by all accounts would have made a wonderful companion for John.

However, John's older brother, Charles, objected to the marriage on the grounds that marriage might interfere with the revival movement. Eventually, John accepted his brother's advice and ended the relationship.

Later in life John met a widow named Molly, whom he decided to marry without consulting Charles. But she turned out to be a shrew, an ill-tempered nagger. She was, by all accounts, a miserable woman.

Molly would sell some of John's favorite books when he was on a speaking tour. Sometimes while he was preaching she would shout from the audience, contradicting what he was saying. One day while preaching he said, "I have been accused of every sin in the catalogue except getting drunk." From the back of the auditorium his wife yelled "Why, John Wesley, you know you were drunk just last week!"

John didn't stop preaching, but replied, "Thank God, that completes the catalogue!" and went on with his sermon as though nothing had happened.

On one occasion Molly became so angry with him that she grabbed him by the hair and dragged him around the room. (He weighed only 120 pounds, she considerably more.)

/esley reacted calmly, never laying
. hand on her to avenge himself. Here
was an example of someone in whom
the grace of God had done a mighty
work!

John learned that conflicts are
opportunities for personal growth.
Blessed are those who use their conflicts as an opportunity to grow together rather than be torn apart. The
rewards for suffering—even marital
suffering—are given to those who
persevere.

Notes

1. This figure, commonly reported in the
   news media, may be low. In a recent study,
   John Powell at Michigan State University
   reported that 38 percent of women inter-
   viewed had been sexually abused by an
   adult or family member by age eighteen
   (as reported in Dan Allender, *The Wounded
   Heart* [Colorado Springs, NavPress, 1990],
   back cover).
2. William Grudem, *Recovering Biblical Man-
   hood and Womanhood* (Wheaton, Ill.: Cross-
   way Books, 1991), p. 195.

Moody Press, a ministry of the Moody Bible
Institute, is designed for education, evangeli-
zation, and edification. If we may assist you
in knowing more about Christ and the Christian life, please write us without obligation:
Moody Press, c/o MLM, Chicago, Illinois 60610.